CITIES THROUGH TIME

Paris

A photographic exploration of how the
city has developed and changed

ANNE ROONEY

Chrysalis Children's Books

First published in the UK in 2005 by
Chrysalis Children's Books
An imprint of Chrysalis Books Group Plc
The Chrysalis Building, Bramley Road,
London W10 6SP

ISBN 1 84458 356 2

British Library Cataloguing in Publication Data for this book
is available from the British Library.

Anne Rooney has asserted her right under the Copyright,
Design and Patents Act 1988 to be identified as the
author of this work.

Contact Anne Rooney by e-mail (anne@annerooney.co.uk)
or visit her website (www.annerooney.co.uk).

Associate Publisher Joyce Bentley
Editorial Manager Rasha Elsaeed
Project Editor Leon Gray
Editorial Assistant Camilla Lloyd
Consultant Jeff Lewis
Designer Alix Wood
Illustrator Mark Walker
Picture Researcher Jamie Dikomite

Printed in China

10 9 8 7 6 5 4 3 2 1

Read Regular, READ SMALLCAPS and Read Space;
European Community Design Registration 2003
and Copyright © Natascha Frensch 2001-2004
Read Medium, **Read Black** and *Read Slanted*
Copyright © Natascha Frensch 2003-2004

READ™ is a revolutionary new typeface that will
enhance children's understanding through clear, easily
recognisable character shapes. With its evenly spaced
and carefully designed characters, READ™ will help
children at all stages to improve their literacy skills,
and is ideal for young readers, reluctant readers
and especially children with dyslexia.

Picture Acknowledgments
All reasonable efforts have been made to ensure the
reproduction of content has been done with the consent
of copyright holders. If you are aware of any unintentional
omissions please contact the publishers directly so that any
necessary corrections may be made for future editions.

T=Top, B=Bottom, L=Left, R=Right, C=Centre
British Library: 5R Maps K TopLXIV.33
Corbis: 21T Dave Bartruff; 23L Adam Woolfitt
Photothèque des Musées de la Ville de Paris: BC C, 16B
Photothèque des Musées de la Ville de Paris/Cliché: 4
Briant; 6, 26T Ladet; 8T Toumazet; FC TL, BC TL, 8B, 12B,
16T, 24, 28T, 28BL Joffre; 10T Jean-Marc Moser; 10B, 18B
Lifermann; 12T Andreani; FC B, 14 Habouzit; 18T, 22, 26B
Degraces; 20 Andreani; 28BR Pierrain
Science Photo Library: 5L CNES, 1993 DISTRIBUTION
SPOT IMAGE
Simon Clay/Chrysalis Image Library: FC TR, FC C, BC TR, 1, 2,
3, 7R, 9, 11, 13, 15, 17, 19, 21B, 23R, 25, 27, 29, 31

CONTENTS

People have lived in the area that is now Paris for more than two thousand years. Today, it is one of the most important and attractive cities in Europe – an artistic centre lived in and loved by artists and authors from around the world.

Then and now

Paris has been home to Gauls, Romans, Vikings and finally the Franks. France was ruled by a king until the French Revolution in 1789. After a decade of chaos, Napoleon Bonaparte took over France and made himself emperor.

Some parts of Paris still follow the Roman street plan, but the city has also seen a lot of change. Napoleon III ruled France between 1852 and 1871. He had large parts of Paris rebuilt. Most of the narrow, winding medieval streets were transformed into wide, tree-lined boulevards. Many of these survive today because they are wide enough for modern traffic.

Napoleon III was the last unelected ruler of France. The country became an official republic in 1871, following the Franco-Prussian War.

Rue St Bon, c.1906. Some medieval back streets still survive in Paris today

Time line

c.300 BCE Celtic Gauls known as the Parisii settle in the area

53 BCE Paris falls to Julius Caesar and becomes Roman Lutetia

c.800–1100 Vikings invade northern France

1253 Robert de Sorbon founds the Sorbonne, the University of Paris

1420–1436 English occupy Paris

1429 Jeanne d'Arc killed in the battle to capture Paris from the English

1572 Massacre of St Bartholomew – thousands killed in religious riots

4

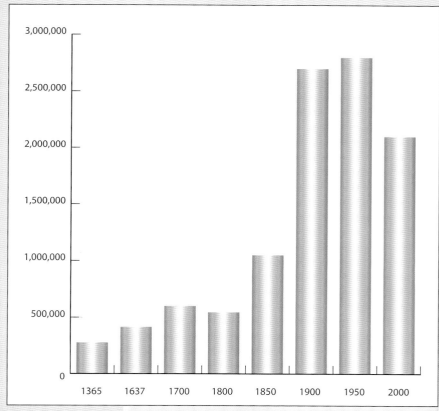

The population of central Paris has grown from 275,000 in 1365 to 2.1 million in 2000

How to use this book

In this book you will find photos of Paris as it was in the past and as it is now. There are questions about the photos to get you to look at and think about them carefully. You may need to do some research to answer some of the questions. You might be able to use:

- encyclopaedias
- CD-ROMs
- reference books
- the Internet.

Page 30 lists useful websites and some films you might like to watch, which show Paris at different times.

A modern satellite image of Paris

A map of Paris dating from 1765

1789 Start of the French Revolution

1804 Napoleon Bonaparte crowned Emperor of France

1851–1868 Architect and engineer Baron X Haussmann rebuilds medieval centre of Paris

1870 Paris under siege during the Franco-Prussian war

1871 Uprising overthrows the French government and France becomes a republic

1940–1944 German troops occupy Paris

1981–1995 President François Mitterrand authorises large-scale architectural projects in the city

The brilliant French engineer Gustave Eiffel designed the Eiffel Tower for the Universal Exhibition in 1889. When it was built, the Eiffel Tower was the tallest structure in the world, standing more than 300 metres tall. The Eiffel Tower was built to last for twenty years, but it is still standing. It is now one of the most famous landmarks in France and a popular tourist attraction.

Back in time

- Look carefully at all the photos of the Eiffel Tower on these two pages. Has the area around the tower changed since 1889?
- Today, you can take a lift to the top of the Eiffel Tower. How do you think the city would look from the top of the Eiffel Tower?

- The old photos below show how the Eiffel Tower was built. Do you think all buildings are built in this way? Compare it with buildings you have seen being built in your local area.
- Many Parisians complained about the Eiffel Tower when it was being built. Why do you think this was?

The Eiffel Tower was built between 1887 and 1889

Mark of remembrance

Landmarks are often made to mark special events. Some structures, such as the Eiffel Tower, are only intended to be temporary. They are usually taken down after the event. Others are built to last.

- Do landmarks such as the Eiffel Tower help people think about or understand past events?
- Find out about a landmark or monument in your local area. When and why was it made? Is it used for anything today?
- Find out what people did to celebrate the new millennium in 2000 in your local area. Are there any lasting monuments? Were there events or celebrations at the time?

Investigate

Imagine that you have been asked to plan a local landmark to mark a special occasion. It could be a structure such as a fountain or a statue, something useful such as a hospital or a library or something people can enjoy such as a playground or park. Draw a design for your landmark, and explain why it will make a good memorial for the special occasion.

Eiffel Tower

Between 1870 and 1871, France was at war with Prussia (part of present-day Germany). In September 1870, Paris was besieged by Prussian soldiers. The Parisians suffered terrible starvation and disease. After the war, the French overthrew their government, and France became a republic. Seventy years later, Paris was occupied again by German troops during World War II (1939–1945).

German troops in Paris, 1940

City under siege

- What is the most obvious difference between the old and new photos taken from Butte Montmartre?
- Why do you think the hilltop at Montmartre was so important to the French army during the 1870 siege?

- What are the two tallest buildings in the new photo? What types of buildings are the tallest in the old photo?
- How did the machinery used in war change between 1871 and 1940 (shown in the photo above)?

Butte Montmartre, 1871

Waging wars

France has fought many wars on its own territory.

- Look at the position of France on a political map of Europe. Why do you think that so many wars have been fought on French land?

During a siege, enemy troops encircle a town or city and no one can get in or out.

- What types of problems would this create for the people who live there?
- How would it be different to live in a city under siege compared to a city occupied by the enemy?

Warfare has changed a lot since the Franco-Prussian War and World War II.

- Think about some news reports of a recent war. In what ways have the machinery and weapons of warfare changed since 1870?

Investigate

Imagine that you are living in Paris during the siege of 1870. The only way to deliver letters to friends and family outside the city is by hot air balloons that are built in some of the railway stations of Paris. Write a letter that will be carried outside Paris by one of these balloons. Try to describe what your life is like, what problems you face and how life has changed since the siege started.

Butte Montmartre

9

Steam trains ran on the first railway lines into Paris. Compared to modern electric trains, these early steam trains were very noisy and smelly. Trains remain one of the most popular ways of travelling in France, and many high-speed lines run across the country. The Gare St Lazare is one of the main stations in Paris. It is used by thousands of commuters every day and links directly with the Métro – the Paris underground system.

Gare St Lazare, late 1880s

Train travel

- What differences can you see in the old and new photos of Gare St Lazare? Can you spot any similarities?

- How do the railway carriages in the old photo of Gare St Lazare differ from the carriages in the new photo?

- How would it feel different to be in a railway station in the 1880s compared to today? Think about the smells, the sounds and the things you might expect to see in the station.

- What things have changed and what has stayed the same in the old and new photos of Odéon Métro station?

- What are the people doing in the old photo of the Odéon Métro?

Odéon Métro station during flooding, 1910

Moving around

New methods of transport have become available since the 1880s, but others are no longer in use. Before the Métro was built around 1900, people travelled in Paris using buses, river boats and trams.

○ Most of the world's major cities have an underground train system like the Paris Métro. What are the advantages of an underground system in a city?

○ Can you think of some methods of transport available now that people did not have in 1900? What are the advantages and disadvantages of the different methods of transport?

○ How do you prefer to travel around the place in which you live?

Investigate

Find out about the different ways of travelling between London and Paris. Look for ways of going by train, plane, boat, or car. Make a chart to display in the window of a travel agent, comparing the distance, cost and time it takes for each mode of transport. Which way would you prefer to travel between the two cities and why?

Gare St Lazare

Odéon Métro station

Paris is built on the River Seine. The river has always been very important and was used for transport for centuries. The Romans built the first bridges over the Seine. The early photo of the quayside by Pont Neuf shows people repairing mattresses. (Pont is the French word for bridge.) The early photo of Pont Marie shows bathing cabins and the floating laundries where washerwomen washed people's clothes and bedding.

Pont Marie

Life on the river

- How does the quayside at Pont Neuf look different in the old and new photos? What are people doing in the new photo?
- What kind of boat can you see on the river in the new photo of Pont Marie? (There is another picture of a boat like this on page 19.)
- What kind of boats can you see in the old photo of Pont Marie? How are these boats being used?

Pont Neuf

Using the river

Many of the world's major cities are built along rivers. Long before the days of railways and lorries, rivers offered a vital way of transporting goods and people. River traffic is still very important in some countries. People use rivers in many other ways, too.

- Is there a river near you? Who uses it? Are there any boats on the river? What are they used for?
- What other things do people do on or near the river? Do you think the river was used in the same way in the past?
- Why has the way people use rivers changed?

Investigate

Imagine that you are writing a brochure for tourists visiting a river in your local area. Explain what the river was used for in the past. What can people do there now? If there are boat trips on the river, find out the times and prices. Make up the details if you cannot find out the information. Draw some pictures to illustrate your brochure.

Pont Marie

Pont Neuf

Rue du Faubourg St Denis is one of the oldest streets in Paris. The arch in the background of the two photos is the St Denis arch. It was built in 1672 in honour of King Louis XIV. In the late 19th century, Rue du Faubourg St Denis was a busy road leading into the centre of Paris. Today, it is still a very busy street next to a lively market area.

Street scenes

- How have the scenes changed in the two photos of Rue du Faubourg St Denis? What is still the same?
- How different would it feel to be in Rue du Faubourg St Denis when the older photo was taken? Think about the sounds and smells as well as what you can see in the photo.

- What are the people doing in the street in the two photos? How have the clothes people wear changed?
- How are the vehicles different in the old and new photos of Rue de Faubourg St Denis?
- What are the posts for along the edge of the street in the new photo?

Rue du Faubourg St Denis

Life on the street

On a warm day in Paris, many people like to sit in roadside cafés, drinking coffee and watching people pass by. Entertainers often put on shows and many people stop to watch. Other people like to look at the displays in shop windows.

- What do people like to do in the streets near where you live?
- Has this changed in the last hundred years?
- How would a busy street in your local area look different from Rue du Faubourg St Denis today?
- Why were there walls with gates around cities? Are there any city walls or gates in a city near you? Find out when and why they were they built.

Investigate

Pick out one person you can see clearly in the old photo of Rue du Faubourg St Denis. It could be one of the people driving a horse-drawn cart or it could be someone walking down the street. Imagine what it might be like to be them. What are they doing in Rue du Faubourg St Denis? What kind of job do they have? Are they rich or poor? Pretend to be that person. Imagine that when you get home you have to tell someone what you have been doing that day. Write down what you would say or record your thoughts on a tape recorder.

Rue du Faubourg St Denis

Parisians like to buy their food from open-air markets such as the one in the Place St Médard. In the past, the markets opened every weekday. Today, each district of Paris has a fresh food market at least once a week. There has been a bird market in Paris since medieval times. Today, it takes place on Sundays and also sells other small pets.

Place St Médard, 1898

Market life

- Look at the people in the old and new photos of the bird market? What clothes are they wearing? Can you tell whether they are rich or poor?
- What differences can you see in the old and new photos of the Place St Médard? Do you think people buy the same foods in the market now as they did when the old photo was taken?
- How are the people in the Place St Médard carrying their shopping? How do people carry their shopping now?

Bird market, Île de la Cité, 1890s

16

Place St Médard

Streets of change

In the past, most people used to visit several different market stalls to get their shopping. Today, most people do their shopping in supermarkets and shopping centres.

⬤ Are there markets in your local area? What sort of things do they sell?
⬤ Have supermarkets and shopping centres changed the ways in which people shop and what they buy? Have these places made it easier to do the shopping?

Now the traders in the bird market at Île de la Cité must have proper certificates and licenses to sell animals. All the animals they sell must be well looked after and bred or imported responsibly.

⬤ Is there a market in your local area where people buy and sell animals? Who goes there?
⬤ Have the ways in which people treat animals changed over the last hundred years? How?

Investigate

Make up a plan of the market in Place St Médard as it might have been in 1898. Label each stall to show what it sells. Now draw a plan of a modern market and label it. Base it on a real market you have been to. How are the things sold on the stalls different?

Bird market, Île de la Cité

Paris was brought to a standstill during terrible floods in 1910. The Métro was put out of action from January until April, the River Seine rose by more than 8 metres, and many streets and buildings were flooded. The photo on page 10 shows the flooding at Odéon Métro station in 1910.

Swollen river

- What are people doing in the old photo of Rue de Lyon?
- What do you think the man with the white stick is doing?
- What are the buildings being used for in the recent photo of Rue de Lyon? Do you think they were used in the same way in 1910 during the floods? How would this affect the people of Paris?

- What differences can you notice in the old and new photos of Pont de l'Alma?
- Why are there no boats on the river in the old photo?
- Why are there so many people lining the river banks in the old photo?
- What do you think the river was like during the floods of 1910?

Rue de Lyon flooded, 1910

Inset: Pont de l'Alma during flooding, 1910

Flood damage

When a river bursts its banks in a city, it can cause a lot of damage. Buildings may collapse. If sewers flood, sewage spills out into the streets. Electricity and gas can also be cut off.

- What other types of natural disasters and disasters caused by people have you heard about recently?
- What effects do you think the disaster might have had on the people living in the area?
- What happened after the disaster?

Investigate

Imagine that you lived in Paris during the floods of 1910. You are being interviewed for a radio programme and asked to recount your memories about the floods. Work with a friend to record the interview. How did the floods affect you personally? Could you still go to school or visit your friends? Was your house or apartment flooded? How did you move around the city and get food during the floods?

Pont de l'Alma

Rue de Lyon

The Louvre in the centre of Paris is one of the oldest and most important art galleries in France. The Louvre has two main wings, which enclose the inner courtyard. The Louvre houses many important and famous works of art, including the *Mona Lisa* by the Italian artist, inventor and scientist Leonardo da Vinci.

Art and architecture

- What differences can you see in the old and new photos of the Louvre?
- Why do you think the pyramids in the new photos are made of glass?

The Tuileries Palace, visible in the centre of the old photo, was torn down during the uprising of 1871. In 1989, the glass pyramids were built. The pyramids, designed by the famous architect I. M. Pei, are the new main entrance to the Louvre. Some people complained about the pyramids when they were first built.

- Do you think the courtyard looks better with the gardens shown in the old photo or with the glass pyramids in the recent photo?
- Why do you think people complained about the glass pyramids when the new courtyard opened in 1989?

Inner courtyard of the Louvre, c.1860

Changing styles

Some people think that any changes to old buildings should be in keeping with the style of the buildings themselves. Other people enjoy new architectural styles used alongside old styles.

- Do you know of an old building in your local area that has been changed recently? How has it changed? Do you like the way it looks now?
- Sometimes, buildings change to make them more suitable for modern life. How do you think the inside of the Louvre might have changed?
- What sort of things do people expect to find in modern buildings that were not present in buildings in 1860? Think about public buildings, such as the Louvre, as well as homes, schools and offices.

Investigate

Imagine you are working at the Louvre in 1989. You have been asked to design an invitation for a party to open the new pyramids. Include a description of the pyramids, and explain why they have been built. Further information can be found on the website mentioned on page 30.

The Louvre

Glass pyramid in the inner courtyard of the Louvre

Notre Dame Cathedral was built between 1163 and 1285 to mark the fortune of medieval Paris. The two square towers house the famous cathedral bells. The original stained glass is still in some of the windows, including the big circular window, called a rose window, at the front of the building. Notre Dame Cathedral was neglected in the 18th century and nearly destroyed during the French Revolution.

Notre Dame

Set the scene

Notre Dame Cathedral is the setting of a famous story about a hunchback bell ringer, Quasimodo. *The Hunchback of Notre Dame* by Victor Hugo was published in 1831. After the novel came out, Parisians asked for the cathedral to be restored.

- Look carefully at the old and new photos of Notre Dame. What has changed and what is still the same?
- What is happening to the building in the old photo?
- Why do you think people visited Notre Dame Cathedral in the 19th century?
- What are the people doing in the new photo?
- Do you think people do the same things inside the cathedral?

Different faiths

Catholic Christianity is one of the most important religions in France, but many people follow different faiths.

- Which religions are most common in the country where you live?
- What types of religious buildings are there in your local area?

Notre Dame Cathedral is one of the major tourist attractions in Paris. Tourists can walk up the towers and spire and enjoy the views across the whole of the city.

- Can a place like Notre Dame Cathedral benefit from tourists who want to come because they have heard or read about it? How?

Investigate

In the Middle Ages, stained glass windows were made to tell important stories from the Bible. Representing stories in this way helped people who could not read remember the stories. Find out about an important story from any religion you choose. Using coloured paper or cellophane and black card or paper, make your own stained glass window to tell the story. Try to make the meaning of your picture clear without using any words.

Stained glass of the rose window

Notre Dame

The Luxembourg Gardens are a large public park where people have enjoyed themselves for hundreds of years. Originally, the gardens were part of a private palace called the Palais de Luxembourg, which was built between 1615 and 1627. The gardens are now open to the public.

Places for people

- What are the people doing in the two photos of Luxembourg Gardens?
- Look closely at the old picture below. What are the children playing with outside? Do children still play with the same things? What do you like to play with when you visit the park?
- What are the people in the recent photo of the gardens doing?

Look at the new photo of Les Halles Market at the top of page 27.

- Les Halles Market and the Luxembourg Gardens are different types of parks. How do they differ?
- How do the children's clothes in the old photo differ from your clothes? Would you like to wear clothes like these?

Luxembourg Gardens, late 19th century

Leisure time

Most towns and cities around the world contain public spaces. Parisians go to these places because most of them live in apartment blocks and do not have a garden.

- Do you go to your local parks or public gardens? What do you do there? What do adults do there?
- Do you think people did the same thing in parks a hundred years ago as you do now?
- Parks and gardens also provide a safe place for wildlife in towns and cities. What animals and plants can you see in the park nearest to you?
- Public spaces are often used for open-air concerts, firework displays and sports events. Are there any places that are used like this in your local area? Find out about the events that you can go to.

Investigate

Imagine that you are one of the children in the old photo of Luxembourg Gardens. You have been out to the gardens for the day. When you get home, you write a letter to a friend describing your day out. Who did you go to the gardens with? How did you get there? What did you do when you got there?

Luxembourg Gardens

ALL CHANGE

Les Halles Market was once the largest fruit and vegetable market in Paris. Market stalls sold fresh produce for nearly eight hundred years. In the 1970s, Les Halles Market was replaced with a public garden and an underground shopping centre, but it is still known as Les Halles Market.

The Gare d'Orsay was built as a railway station for the Universal Exhibition in 1900. It closed down in 1938 because it was too close to the city centre to be useful. In 1978, Gare d'Orsay was restored as an art museum.

Les Halles Market

Different use

- Can you see any similarities between the two photos of Les Halles Market? Why do you think the new structures are built in this way?
- In what ways are the two photos of the Gare d'Orsay different? In what ways are they the same? What are the people doing in the new photo?

Gare d'Orsay, early 20th century

Les Halles Market

Work to leisure

The Gare d'Orsay was originally built as a railway station. Today, it is still a public place, but it is not used for the same purpose. The building remains, but the interior is organised in a completely different way. On the other hand, Les Halles Market was demolished and the building totally replaced. Both the Gare d'Orsay and Les Halles Market were once working places – a train station and a market. They are now used solely for leisure activities.

- Are there any buildings or places in your local area that were once used for work but are now used for leisure activities? What has happened to the activities that were originally carried out there?
- Has this made a difference to the people who live and work in the local area? Has it made their lives better or worse?

Investigate

Is there a building or place in your area that has changed its use? Find out about it. Why did it change? Write a report for a local newspaper. Describe how the place has changed and what effect this has had on people who live or work in the area.

Musée d'Orsay

NO CHANGE

Some parts of Paris have changed very little. The Gare du Nord was built in 1863 to serve passengers travelling to and from northern France and remains so today. The Place Vendôme was built between 1687 and 1721. The column was made later using 2,000 canons captured from Napoleon's enemies. The Place Vendôme was destroyed during the uprising in 1871 but then rebuilt. The statue on the top of the column has changed several times. The Cour de Rohan is a group of grand houses built in the 17th century. Some of the most luxurious apartments in the city are here.

Gare du Nord, early 20th century

Staying the same

- Why do you think each of the places in these photos has remained the same?
- Can you think of any reason why they might change in the future?
- How do you think the insides of each building might have changed?

Place Vendôme, before 1871

Cour de Rohan

Gare du Nord

Investigate

Are there any buildings or places in your local area that have changed very little in the last two hundred years? Choose one place you know has not changed. Find out when it was built and what it is used for. Imagine what it might look like a hundred years from now. Draw a picture of the place and the surrounding area. What do you think will change? What type of vehicles and clothes do you think people might have?

Restoration

Old buildings are often restored to make them more comfortable and suit the needs of the people using them now.

- How old are the houses or apartments in your local area?
- Do you know any very old houses?

- How are they different inside today from how they would have been when they were first built?
- Would you like to live in an old house? What advantages might there be to living in an old house? Would there be any disadvantages?

Cour de Rohan

Place Vendôme

On the map

This map shows where the places photographed in the book are in Paris.

1   Butte Montmartre (pages 8, 9)
2   Cour de Rohan (pages 28, 29)
3   Eiffel Tower (pages 6, 7)
4   Gare du Nord (pages 28, 29)
5   Gare St Lazare (pages 10, 11)
6   Île de la Cité (pages 16, 17)
7   Les Halles Market (pages 26, 27)
8   Louvre (pages 20, 21)
9   Luxembourg Gardens
       (pages 24, 25)
10   Musée d'Orsay (page 27)
11   Notre Dame (pages 22, 23)
12   Odéon Métro (pages 10, 11)
13   Pont de l'Alma (pages 18, 19)
14   Pont Marie (pages 12, 13)
15   Pont Neuf (pages 12, 13)
16   Place St Médard (pages 16, 17)
17   Place Vendôme (pages 28, 29)
18   Rue de Lyon (pages 18, 19)
19   Rue du Faubourg St Denis
       (pages 14, 15)
20   Rue St Bon (page 4)

At the movies

There have been lots of movies set in Paris.
To get a glimpse of life in Paris in the past,
watch:

An American in Paris.
Directed by Vincente Minnelli, 1951.

Funny Face.
Directed by Stanley Donen, 1957.

The Hunchback of Notre Dame.
Directed by Wallace Worsley, 1923.

Madeline.
Directed by Daisy von Scherler Mayer, 1998.

On the Internet

A history of Paris and some of its most
famous buildings:
www.ibiblio.org/wm/paris/hist/

Find out more about the Louvre at:
www.louvre.fr/louvrea.htm

Find out more about the Eiffel Tower at:
www.tour-eiffel.fr/teiffel/uk

Find out more about bridges in Paris at:
www.paris.fr/EN/Visiting/bridges.asp

Find out more about Notre Dame
cathedral at:
www.elore.com/Gothic/History/
Overview/paris.htm

advantage something useful or good

architect person who designs buildings

architectural to do with buildings

besieged surrounded by enemy troops

boulevard wide avenue

commuter person who travels into a city to work

disadvantage something inconvenient or bad

engineer person who works out how to make structures from metal

Gauls people who lived in northern France in early times

leisure time time spent enjoying yourself

luxurious very comfortable and often expensive

massacre killing of a large number of people

memorial something made to remind people of someone or something

Millennium the year 2000, or period of a thousand years

monarchy government or country ruled by a king or queen

monument building or statue made to remind people of a person or event

Nazi Party ruling group in Germany in the 1930s and until 1945

occupy take control of an area with force

protest complain about

republic form of government in which people choose their leader by voting in an election

sewage dirty water and waste

sewer pipes or channels to carry sewage

siege state of surrounding a city or town and not letting people go in and out of it

spire tall tower on a church

temporary not intended to last long

tram vehicle like a bus that runs on metal rails in the ground

unelected not chosen by people in an election

INDEX